THE LIBRARY OF
PIANO
ENTERTAINMENT

THE LIBRARY OF
PIANO
ENTERTAINMENT

To Andrew Rubenoff, the prince of piano entertainment

EDITOR: AMY APPLEBY
EDITORIAL ASSISTANT: ELAINE ADAM
MUSIC RESTORATION AND ENGRAVING: ANNE DENVIR

ORDER NO. AM 980672
US INTERNATIONAL STANDARD BOOK NUMBER: 0.8256.2964.0
UK INTERNATIONAL STANDARD BOOK NUMBER: 1.84449.632.5

EXCLUSIVE DISTRIBUTORS:
MUSIC SALES CORPORATION
257 PARK AVENUE SOUTH, NEW YORK, NY 10010 USA
MUSIC SALES LIMITED
8/9 FRITH STREET, LONDON W1D 3JB ENGLAND
MUSIC SALES PTY. LIMITED
120 ROTHSCHILD STREET, ROSEBERY, SYDNEY, NSW 2018, AUSTRALIA

PRINTED IN THE UNITED STATES OF AMERICA BY
VICKS LITHOGRAPH AND PRINTING CORPORATION

AMSCO PUBLICATIONS
A PART OF THE MUSIC SALES GROUP
NEW YORK/LONDON/PARIS/SYDNEY/COPENHAGEN/BERLIN/TOKYO/MADRID

Contents

GOLDEN HITS AND SHOWSTOPPERS

NOVELTY SOLOS

BLUES AND RAGTIME

After You've Gone

Henry Creamer & J. Turner Layton

Moderato

Ain't We Got Fun

Richard A. Whiting

Moderato

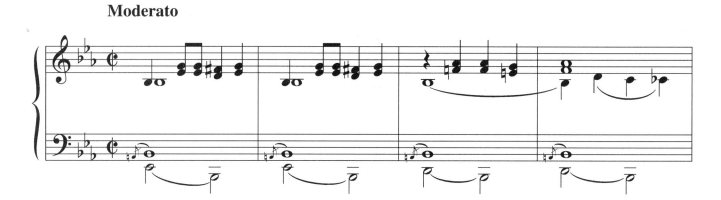

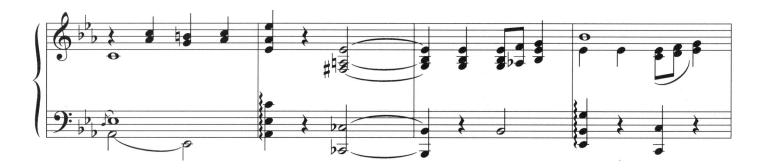

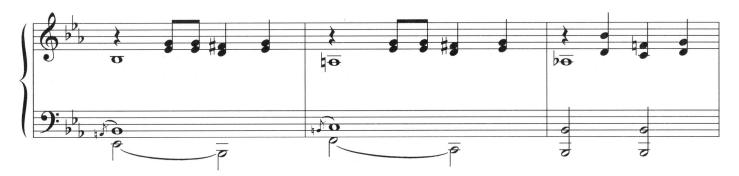

Alexander's Ragtime Band

Irving Berlin

Moderato

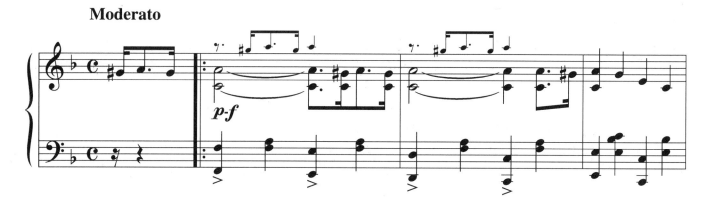

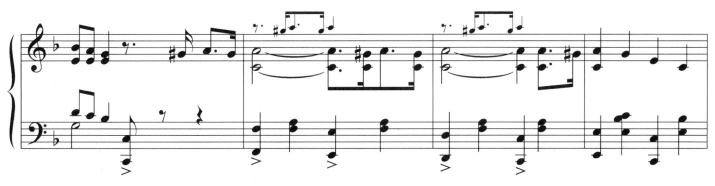

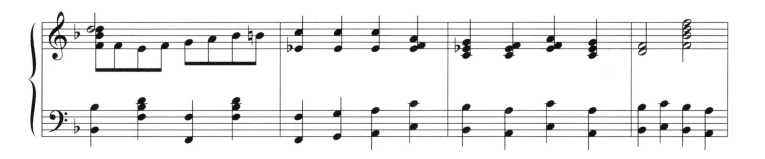

Alice Blue Gown

Harry Tierney

Moderato

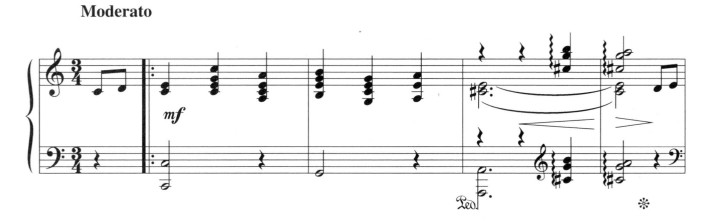

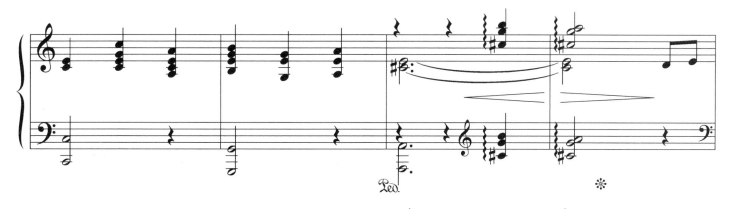

Bill Bailey

Hughie Cannon

Moderato

Carolina in the Morning

Walter Donaldson

Moderato

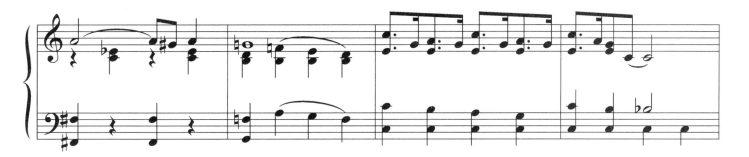

Ciribiribin

Alberto Pestalozza

With movement

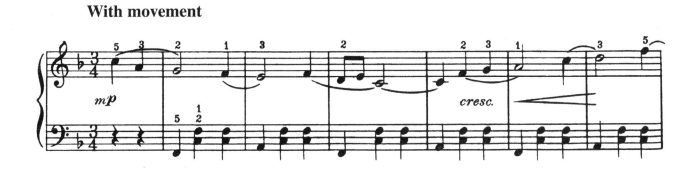

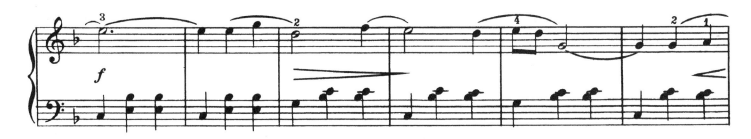

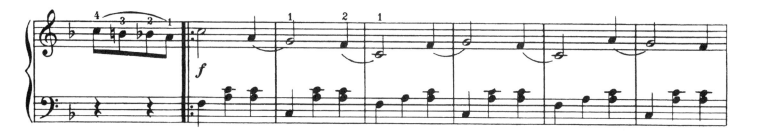

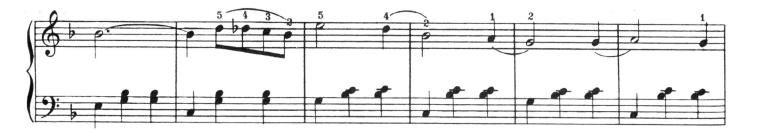

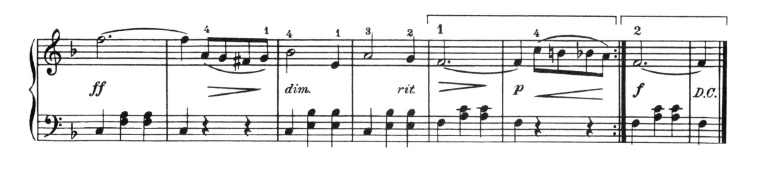

Danny Boy

Traditional Irish air

Gently

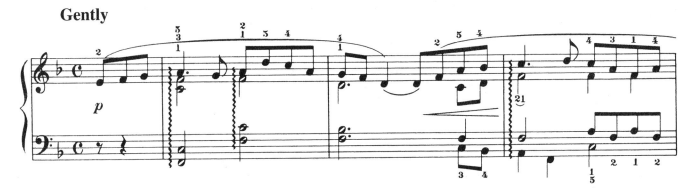

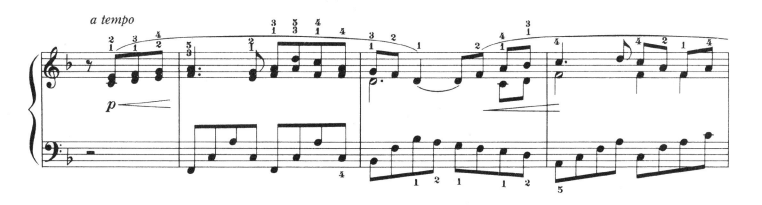

Give My Regards to Broadway

George M. Cohan

Brightly

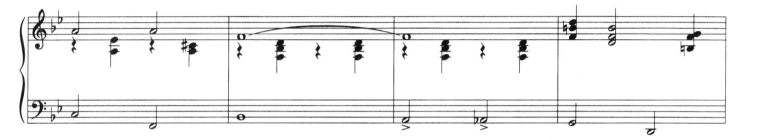

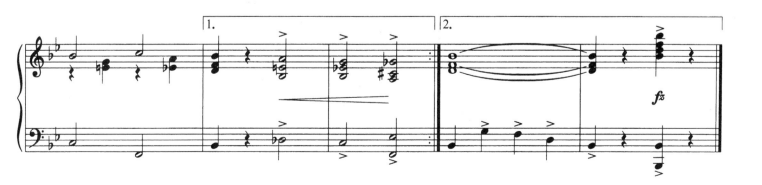

I'll Build a Stairway to Paradise

George Gershwin

With a steady beat

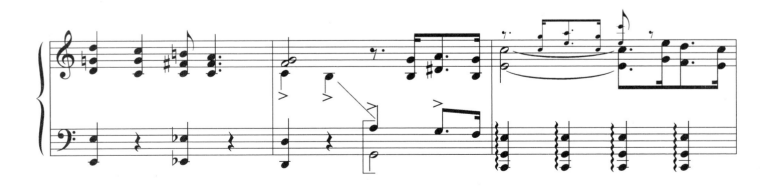

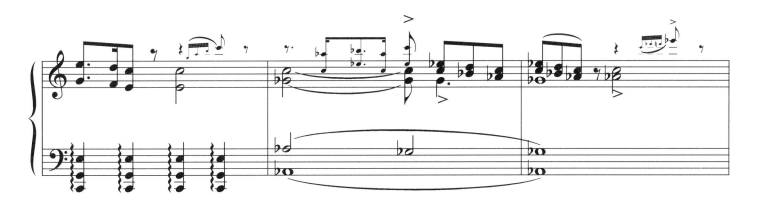

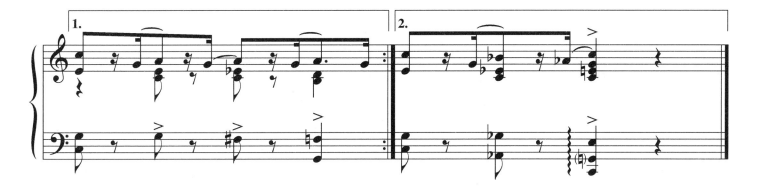

I Love a Piano

Irving Berlin

Allegro moderato

I'm Always Chasing Rainbows

Harry Carroll

Freely

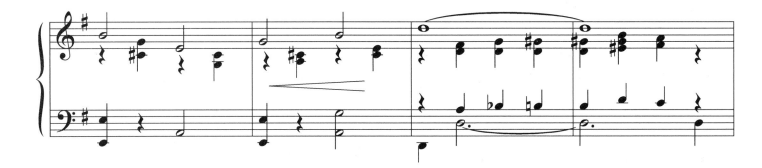

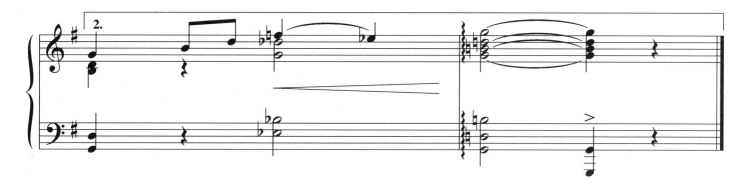

I'm Forever Blowing Bubbles

Jean Kenbrovin & John William Kellette

Moderato

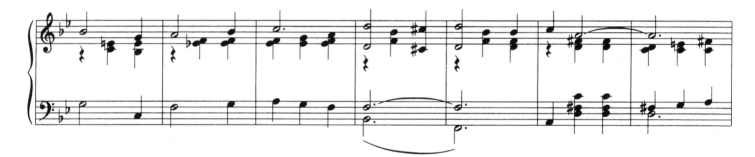

In the Shade of the Old Apple Tree

Egbert van Alstyne

Moderato

Limehouse Blues

Philip Braham

Moderato

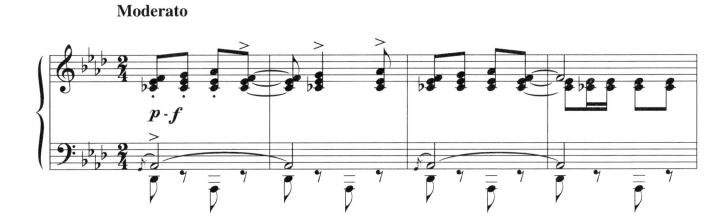

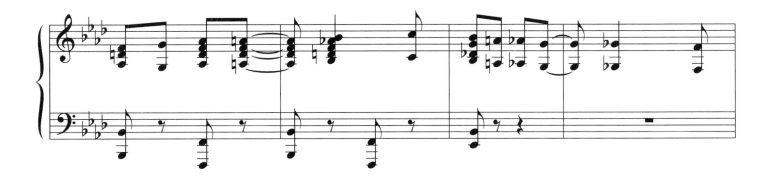

Look for the Silver Lining

Jerome Kern

Moderato

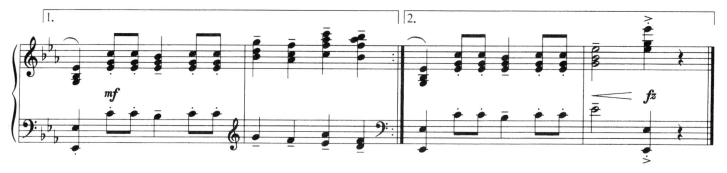

Moonlight Bay

Percy Wenrich

With movement

My Melancholy Baby

Ernie Burnett

Moderato

Play a Simple Melody

Irving Berlin

Moderato

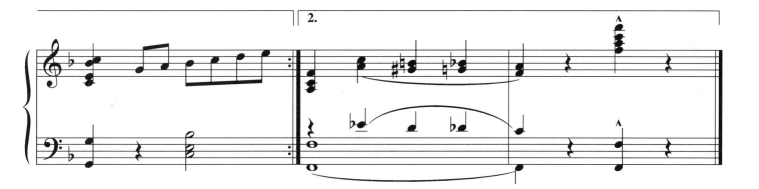

A Pretty Girl Is Like a Melody

Irving Berlin

Moderato

Rock-a-Bye Your Baby with a Dixie Melody

Jean Schwartz

Moderato

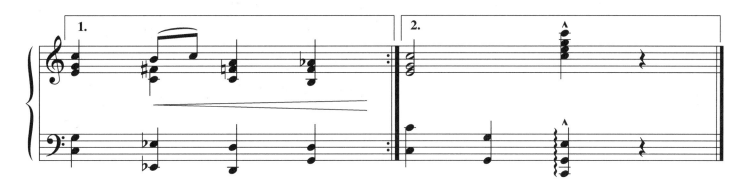

Pretty Baby

Egbert van Alstyne & Tony Jackson

Moderato

Shine On Harvest Moon

Nora Bayes & Jack Norworth

Moderately slow

Some of These Days

Shelton Brooks

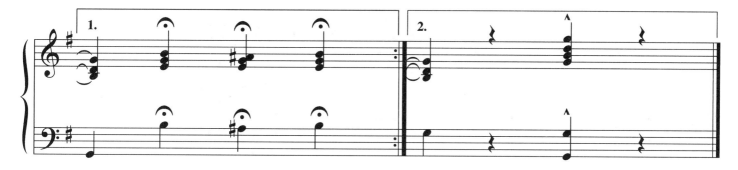

They Didn't Believe Me

Jerome Kern

Gently

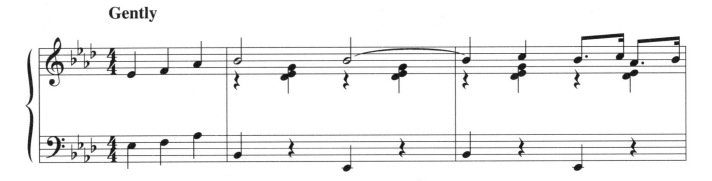

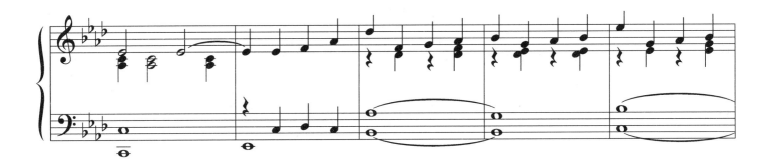

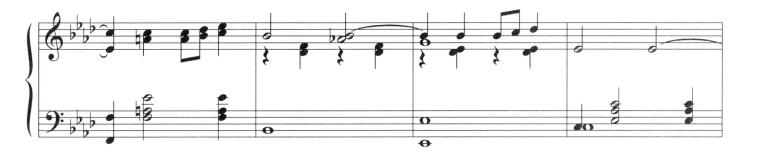

Way Down Yonder in New Orleans

Henry Creamer & J. Turner Layton

Moderato

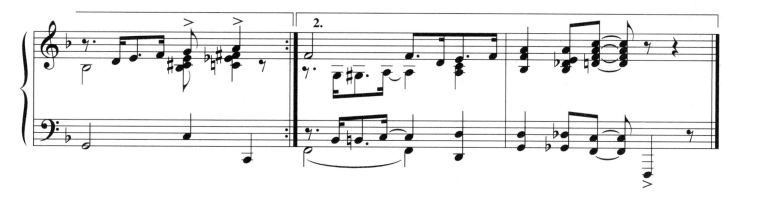

You Made Me Love You

James V. Monaco

Moderato

The Banjo

Louis Moreau Gottschalk

Introduction

Moderato

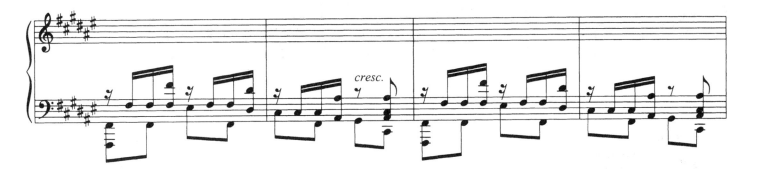

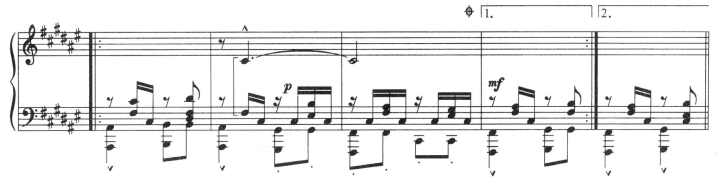

D.S. al 𝄋

Coda

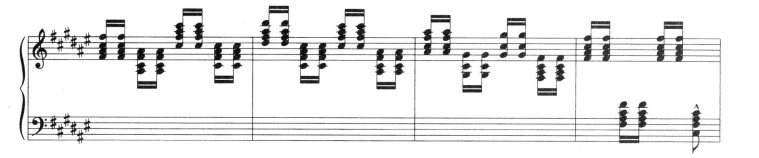

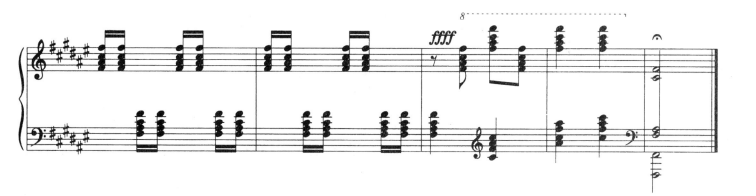

El Choclo

A.G. Villoldo

Moderato

Chopsticks

Arthur de Lulli

Staccato

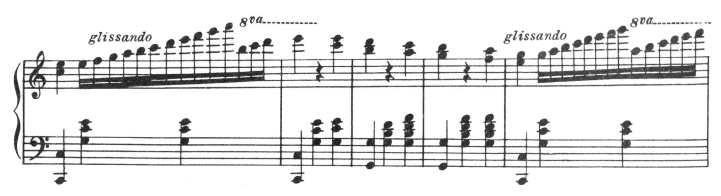

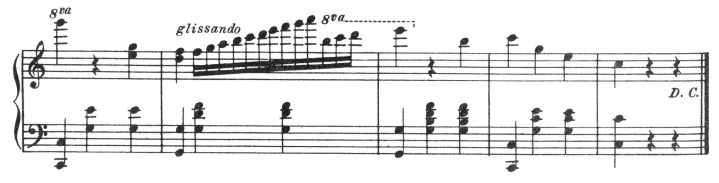

Coaxing the Piano

Zez Confrey

Not too fast

TRIO

Creole Eyes

Louis Moreau Gottschalk

Brilliantly

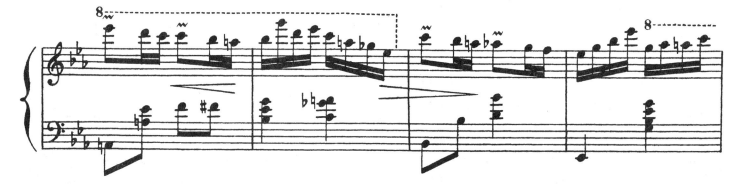

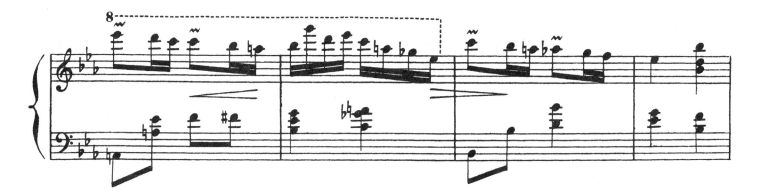

ben misurato

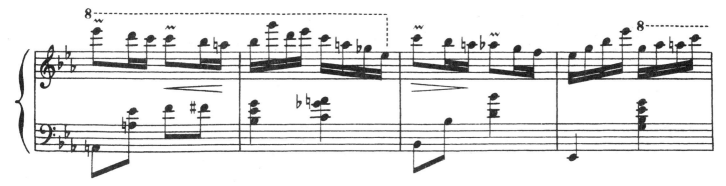

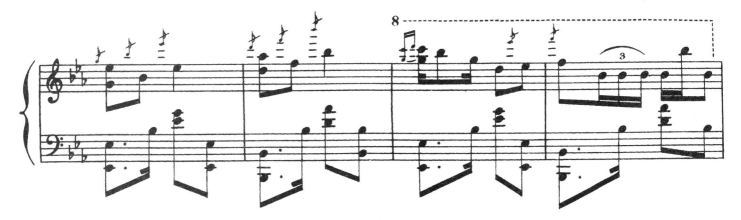

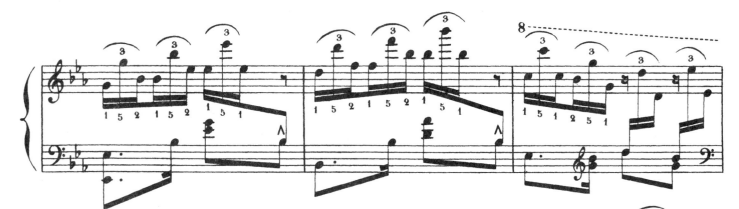

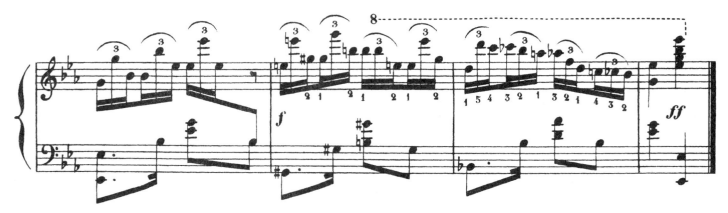

La Cumparsita

G.H. Matos Rodriguez

Slow tango

Entry of the Gladiators

Julius Fucik

Energetico

Trio

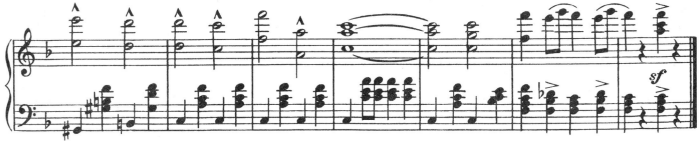

Estudiantina

Emil Waldteufel

INTRODUCTION
Waltz tempo

VALSE
Estudiantina (*Refrain*)

2.

84

3.

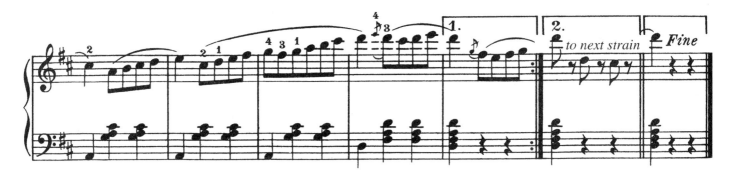

Funeral March of a Marionette

Charles Gounod

Allegretto

The Procession

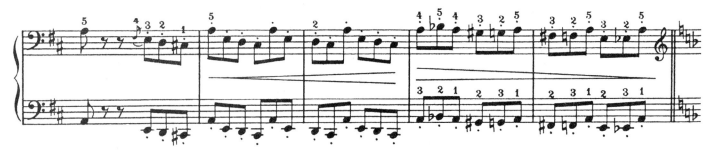

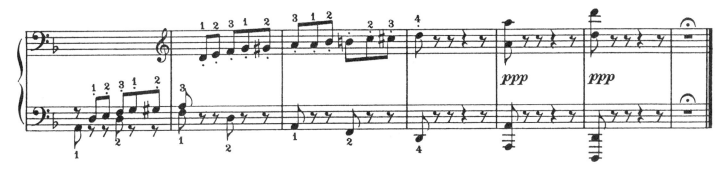

The Golden Wedding

Gabriel-Marie

Moderately slow

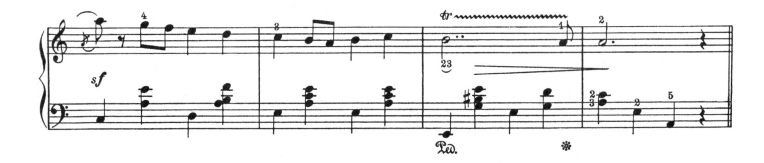

Greenwich Witch

Zez Confrey

Quickly

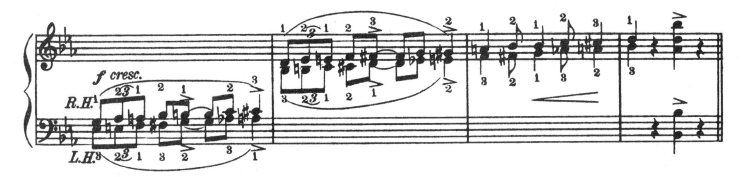

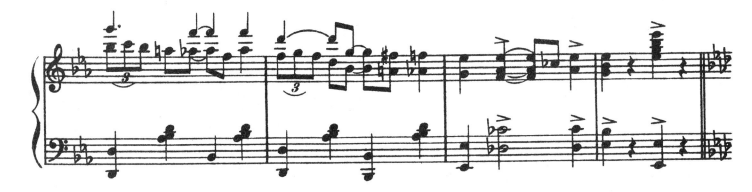

Havah Nagilah

Traditional Hebrew dance

Energetico

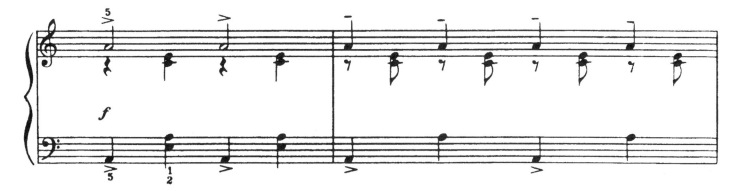

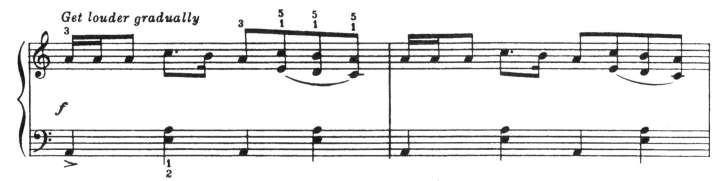

Kitten on the Keys

Zez Confrey

Allegro moderato

TRIO

The Liberty Bell

John Philip Sousa

Moderately

My Pet

Zez Confrey

Moderately fast

Nola

Felix Arndt

Lightly

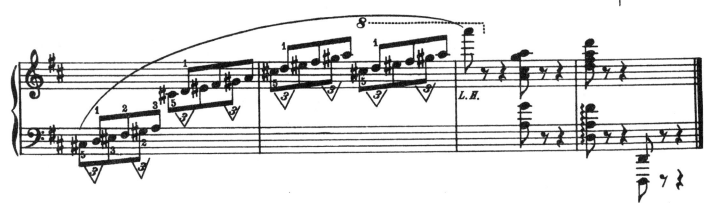

Semper Fidelis

John Philip Sousa

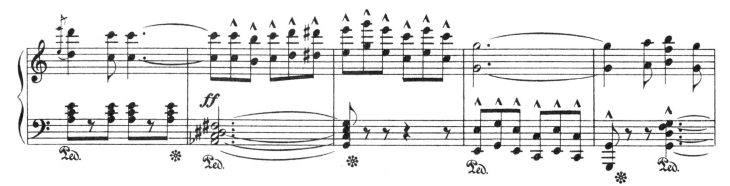

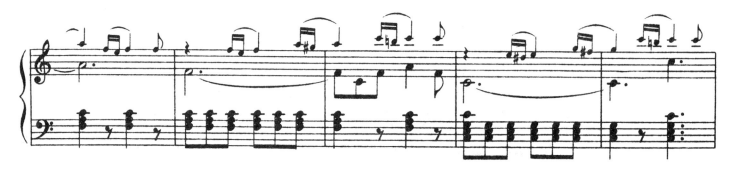

Over the Waves

Juventino Rosas

With movement

Stars and Stripes Forever

John Philip Sousa

Energetico

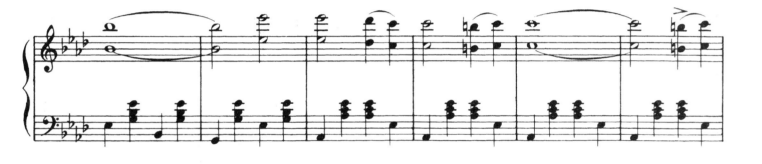

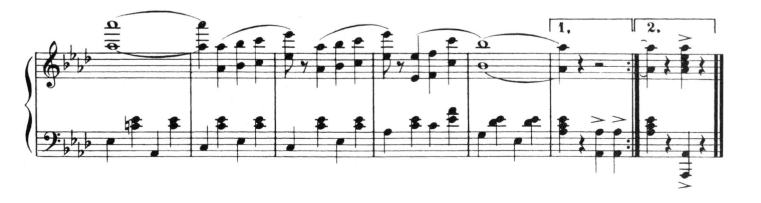

Tango

Isaac Albéniz

Andantino

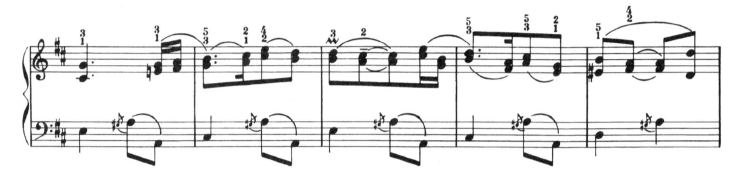

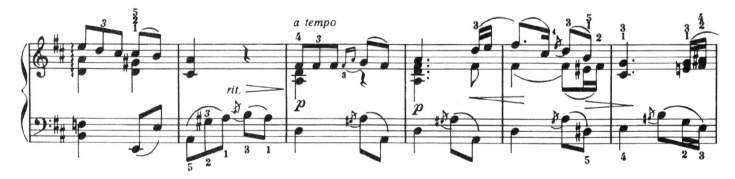

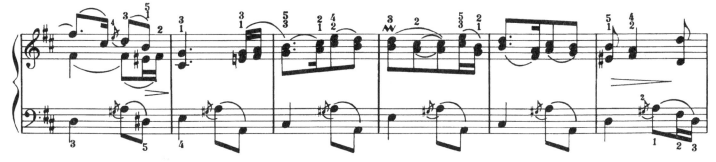

The Teddy Bears' Picnic

John W. Bratton & James B. Kennedy

Allegro moderato

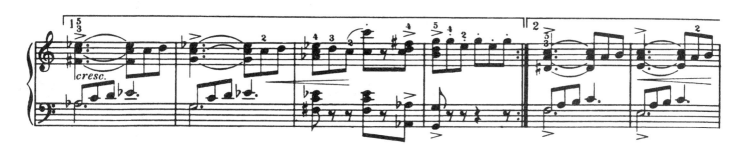

TRIO

The Thunderer

John Philip Sousa

The Washington Post

John Philip Sousa

Moderato

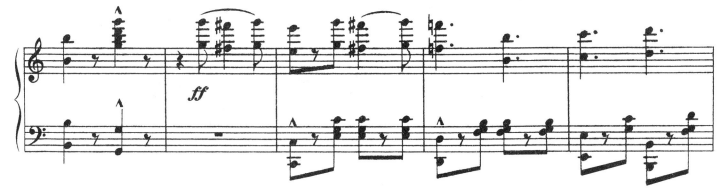

The Whistler and His Dog

Arthur Pryor

Moderato

You Tell 'Em Ivories

Zez Confrey

Allegro moderato

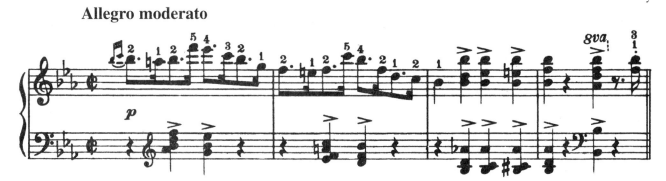

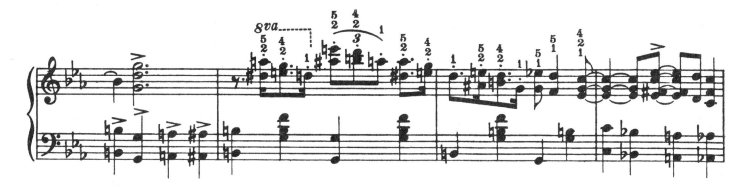

144

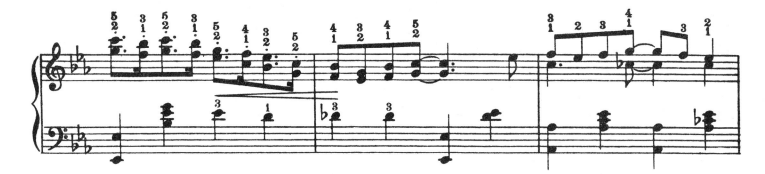

TRIO

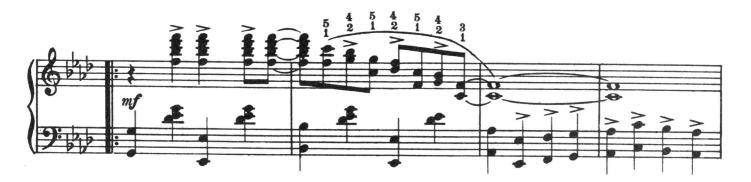

American Beauty Rag

Joseph Lamb

Slow march tempo

Beale Street Blues

W.C. Handy

Moderato

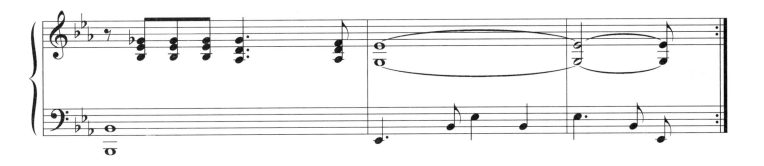

Bugle Call Rag

Eubie Blake

Moderato

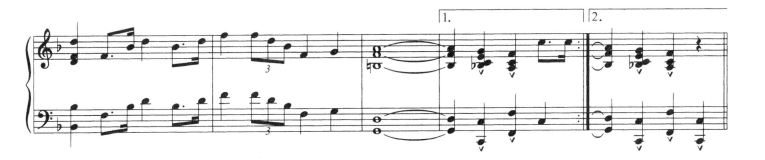

to Coda ⊕

Trio

⊕ **Coda**

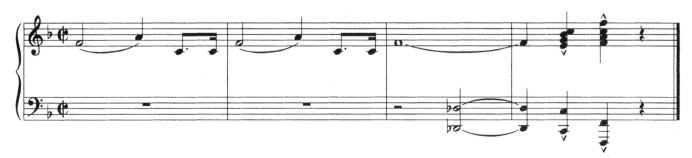

The Chevy Chase

Eubie Blake

Moderato

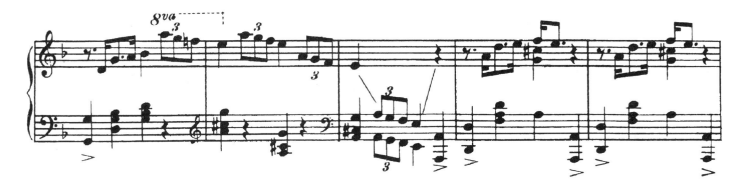

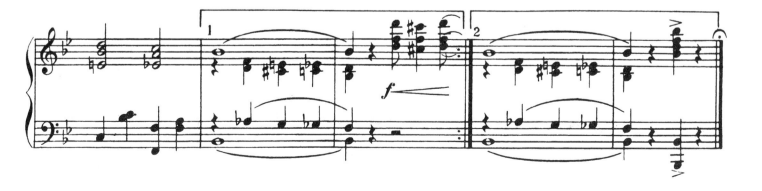

Cabbage Leaf Rag

Les Copeland

Moderato

Dallas Blues

Spencer Williams

Slow blues

The Easy Winners

Scott Joplin

Not fast

The Entertainer

Scott Joplin

Not fast

Fizz Water

Eubie Blake

Moderato

TRIO

175

Golliwog's Cakewalk

Claude Debussy

Allegro guisto

Un peu moins vite

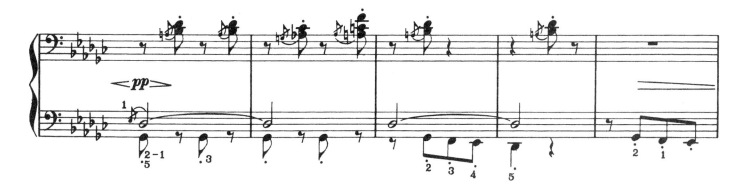

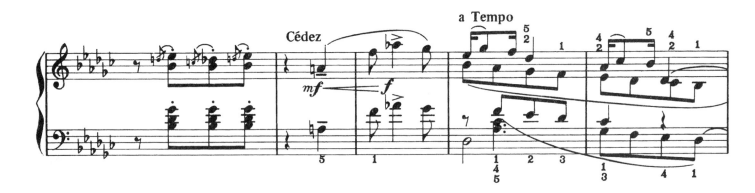

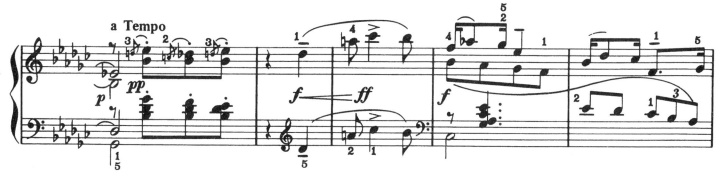

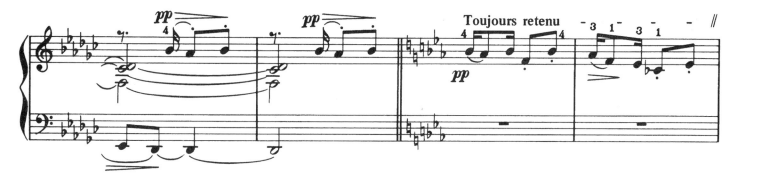

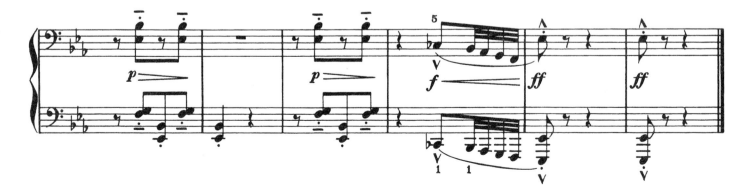

Great Scott Rag

James Scott

Not fast

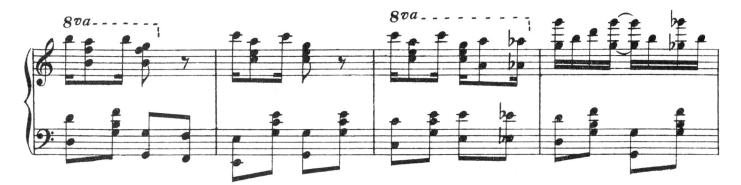

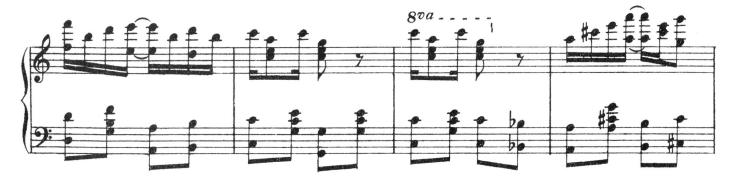

Grace and Beauty

James Scott

Allegro guisto

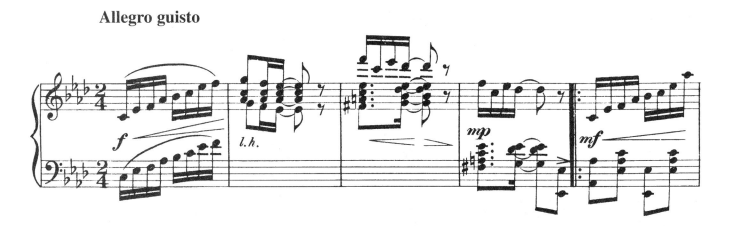

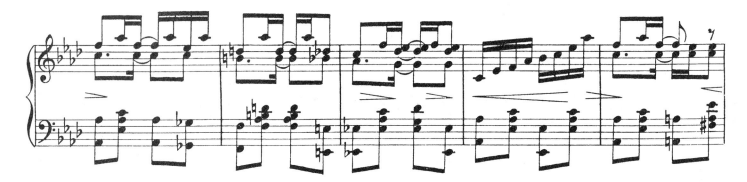

TRIO

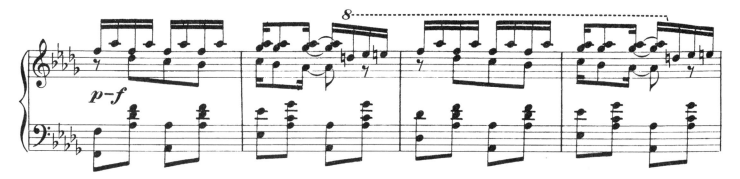

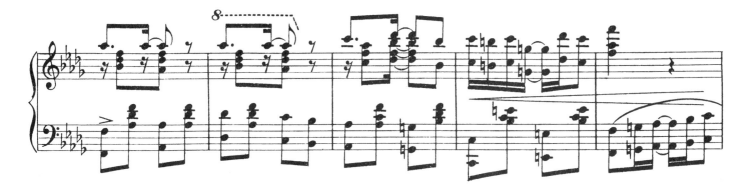

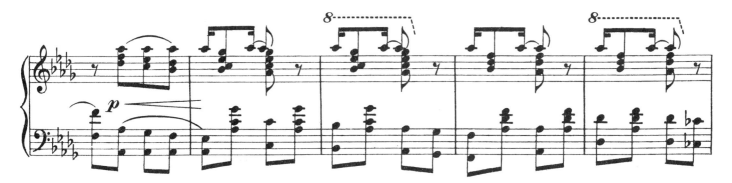

Heliotrope Bouquet

Scott Joplin & Louis Chauvin

Slowly

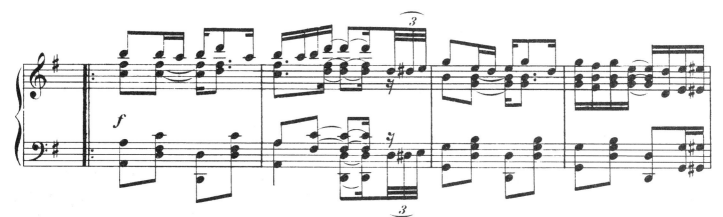

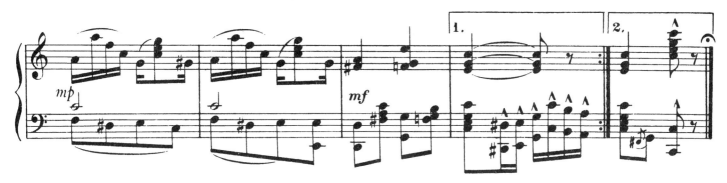

Jelly Roll Blues

Jelly Roll Morton

Moderate blues tempo

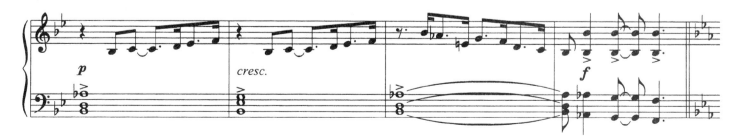

Maple Leaf Rag

Scott Joplin

Moderate blues tempo

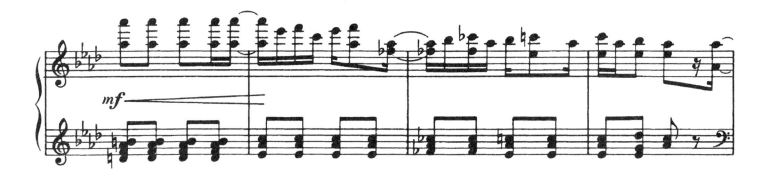

TRIO

The Original Chicago Blues

James White

Moderato

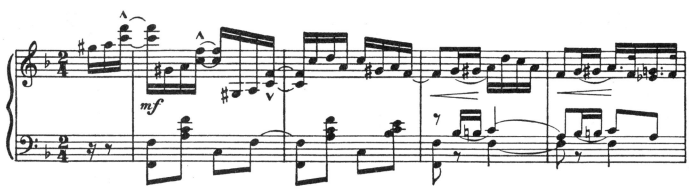

Minstrels

Claude Debussy

Lightly

p les "gruppetti" sur le temps

Cédez **Mouv^t**

Cédez **Mouv^t** (Un peu plus allant)

(très détaché)

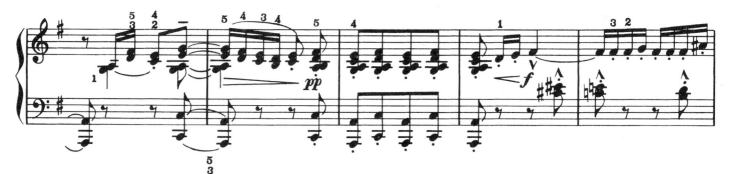

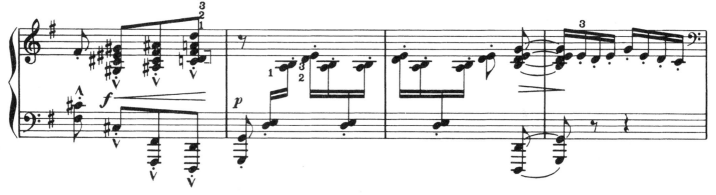

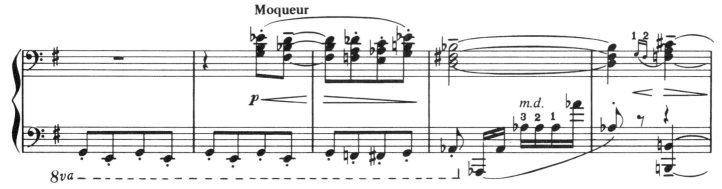

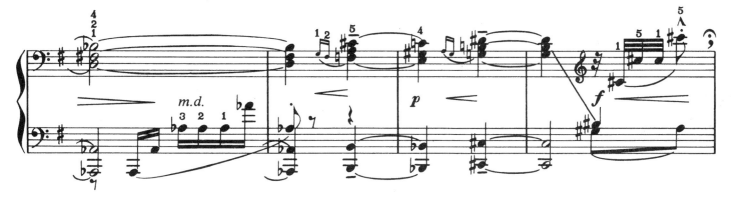

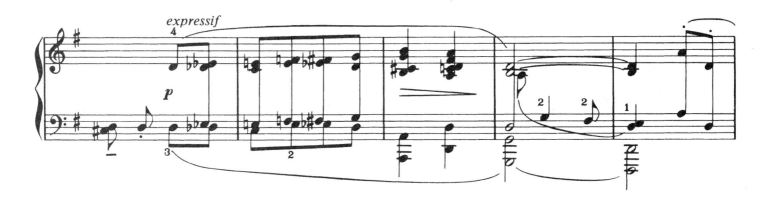

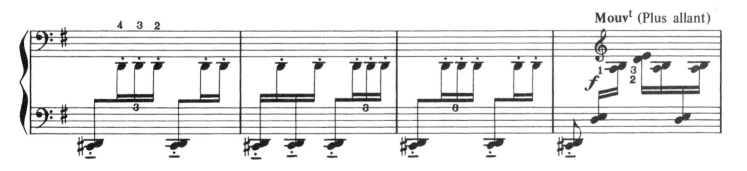

The Music Box Rag

C. Luckyth 'Luckey' Roberts

Moderato

Trio

Pastime Rag No. 3

Artie Matthews

Moderato

Rialto Ripples

George Gershwin

Marcato

Trio

D.S. al fine

Solace

Scott Joplin

Very slow march time

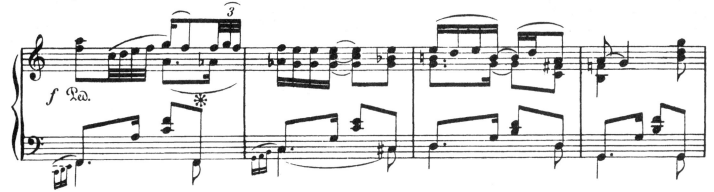

St. Louis Blues

W.C. Handy

Moderato

8va ad. lib.

Chorus

Tiger Rag

D.J. La Rocca

With movement

Sunflower Slow Drag

Scott Joplin & Scott Hayden

Not fast

Swipesy

Scott Joplin & Arthur Marshall

Slowly

Twelfth Street Rag

Euday L. Bowman

Moderato

8

Index